7 SIDES OF THE INHERITANCE

Note: All scriptures are quoted from www.biblegateway.com

Table of contents

INTRODUCTION

We have an inheritance package as God's children with seven blessings in it. However, most believers have not taken advantage of their available inheritance or they have enjoyed just some of the packages. You can have money in the bank and if you don't know about it, you will suffer like other poor people.

God laments that his children perish, not because he has not made provisions available, but because they don't know.

Hosea 4:6
my people are destroyed from lack of knowledge.

Not everything believers were meant to get by using their money. There is another currency, that of the kingdom and if you have it, you can get what the rich in the world are getting with their money and if you have money, you will still get them and save your earthly money for something else.

Isaiah 55:1-2
"Come, all you who are thirsty,

come to the waters;
and you who have no money,
    Come, buy and eat!
Come, buy wine and milk
    without money and without cost.
Why spend money on what is not bread,
    and your labour on what does not satisfy?
Listen, listen to me, and eat what is good,
    and you will delight in the richest of fare.

All children of God have been given equal measure of this currency then from there the choice to increase it or leave it like that is yours. The same way on earth we all have 24-hours, so is the kingdom currency.

Romans 12:3
For I say to every man that is among you, through the grace given unto me, not to think of himself more highly than he ought to think, but to think soberly according as God hath dealt to every man the measure of faith.

There is an inheritance fully paid for by the blood of Jesus. All you have to do is hear about it and take a step to access it. Hearing is the way to increase the faith currency.

Romans 10:17
So then faith comes by hearing, and hearing by the word of God.

Like on earth you give money in exchange for products and services, so it is with the kingdom of heaven, show God your currency of faith and you have the package of the inheritance delivered to you.

Hebrews 11:6
And without faith it is impossible to please God, because anyone who comes to him must believe that he exists and that he rewards those who earnestly seek him.

This is the only way to be ahead of the people of the world and showcase the glory of God. Like it takes time to gather money, so does it take time to gather this kingdom currency.

A believer has to labour in the word of God to find out what the father has made available for them.

1st Timothy 5:17
Let the elders that rule well be counted worthy of double honour, especially those who labour in the Word and doctrine.

Unfortunately many people have chased for money only and their lives have remained ordinary.

Matthew 6:32-33
For the pagans run after all these things, and your heavenly Father knows that you need them. But seek first his kingdom and his righteousness, and all these things will be given to you as well.

It doesn't matter where you are in life or what your condition is, you have an inheritance that can get you out of any situation. You are not disadvantaged in this life. Where the world system has failed, God's system has not.
When God came to the formless earth, he didn't think of creating Adam first so that his son could help him deal with

the mess, he re-created the world and made all provisions available before bringing his son into existence. When Adam was created, he only had to enjoy fellowship with God and take care of the creation. With a simple instruction not to eat from the tree of good and evil, Adam decided to cross boundaries and the king became a slave to satan. The inheritance was all his but he willingly chose death over life.

Genesis 1:31
God saw all that he had made, and it was very good.

Romans 5:14
Nevertheless, death reigned from the time of Adam to the time of Moses, even over those who did not sin by breaking a command, as did Adam, who is a pattern of the one to come.

Luke 4:5-8
The devil led him up to a high place and showed him in an instant all the kingdoms of the world. And he said to him, "I will give you all their authority and splendour; **it has been given to me, and I can give it to anyone I want to.** If you worship me, it will all be yours."

Jesus answered, "It is written: 'Worship the Lord your God and serve him only.'

When he went to deliver a whole nation of Israel out of Egypt captivity, he was not taking them out so that they die in the wilderness, No! He knew where he was taking them. Canaan was the destination he had prepared for the seed of Abraham. All the Israelites had to do was to believe that he had a plan for them which most Israelites found to be hard and they died in the wilderness. Out of a whole nation, only two people entered canaan. That is to say, just because there is an inheritance doesn't mean all will enjoy it.

Numbers 14:26-32
The Lord said to Moses and Aaron: "How long will this wicked community grumble against me? I have heard the complaints of these grumbling Israelites. So tell them, 'As surely as I live, declares the Lord, I will do to you the very thing I heard you say: In this wilderness your bodies will fall—every one of you twenty years old or more who was counted in the census and who has grumbled against me. **Not**

one of you will enter the land I swore with uplifted hand to make your home, except Caleb son of Jephunneh and Joshua son of Nun. As for your children that you said would be taken as plunder, I will bring them in to enjoy the land you have rejected. But as for you, your bodies will fall in this wilderness.

That is the responsible father that we have today. He has finished the salvation package inheritance through Christ and given us access to it. But look at believers, they are suffering the same things the world is suffering and even admiring the world while the world was meant to admire them. What an error!

Ecclesiastes 10:5-7
There is an evil I have seen under the sun,
As an error proceeding from the ruler:
 Folly is set in great dignity,
While the rich sit in a lowly place.
 I have seen servants on horses,
While princes walk on the ground like servants.

Abraham, the father of faith, when he saw problems ,forgot he had an inheritance package and ran to Egypt for help. He knew people there didn't know God therefore he asked his wife to lie that he was her brother. When the wife was taken, you can imagine the sleepless night that Abraham had just knowing his wife was in the arms of another man. The fear of being in the midst of men who didn't know God tormented him. It took God to intervene and repay him back.

Genesis 12:10-20
Now there was a famine in the land, and Abram went down to Egypt to live there for a while because the famine was severe. As he was about to enter Egypt, he said to his wife Sarai, "I know what a beautiful woman you are. When the Egyptians see you, they will say, 'This is his wife.' Then they will kill me but will let you live. Say you are my sister, so that I will be treated well for your sake and my life will be spared because of you."
When Abram came to Egypt, the Egyptians saw that Sarai was a very beautiful woman.And when Pharaoh's officials saw her, they praised her to Pharaoh, and she was taken into his

palace. He treated Abram well for her sake, and Abram acquired sheep and cattle, male and female donkeys, male and female servants, and camels.

But the Lord inflicted serious diseases on Pharaoh and his household because of Abram's wife Sarai. So Pharaoh summoned Abram. "What have you done to me?" he said. "Why didn't you tell me she was your wife? Why did you say, 'She is my sister,' so that I took her to be my wife? Now then, here is your wife. Take her and go!" Then Pharaoh gave orders about Abram to his men, and they sent him on his way, with his wife and everything he had.

That's where most believers are, they have not known or even accessed their inheritance and there is no difference between them and the world. Moses wanted the presence of God so much that he refused to move on with the journey. Why? He knew that was the only thing that would distinguish the Israelites from other nations.

Exodus 33:15-16

Then Moses said to him, "If your Presence does not go with us, do not send us up from here. How will anyone know that you are pleased with me and with your people unless you go with us? What else will distinguish me and your people from all the other people on the face of the earth?"

Don't be comfortable living an ordinary life, push for that realm where the world comes to the brightness of your rising when you take advantage of your inheritance.

Isaiah 60:3
Nations will come to your light,
    and kings to the brightness of your dawn.

The blood of Jesus has paid for it, it's time to access it. Don't be among those who will go to heaven and have their tears wiped when they see the inheritance that was available for them and they didn't use it.

Revelation 21:4

He will wipe away every tear from their eyes, and death shall be no more, neither shall there be mourning, nor crying, nor pain anymore, for the former things have passed away."

Jesus came that you have life and have it to the fullest, don't listen to the lies of satan he is the father of them and a thief of what is yours.

John 10:10
The thief comes only to steal and kill and destroy; I have come that they may have life, and have it to the full.

John 8:44
You belong to your father, the devil, and you want to carry out your father's desires. He was a murderer from the beginning, not holding to the truth, for there is no truth in him. When he lies, he speaks his native language, for he is a liar and the father of lies.

Arise, shine for your time has come. The kingdom has been prepared waiting for you.

Isaiah 60:1
Arise, shine, for your light has come,
    and the glory of the Lord rises upon you.

Matthew 25:34
Then shall the King say unto them on His right hand, 'Come,
ye blessed of My Father, inherit the Kingdom prepared for
you from the foundation of the world.

CHAPTER ONE: POWER AND RICHES

REVELATION 5:12
saying with a loud voice:

"Worthy is the Lamb who was slain
To receive power and riches and wisdom,
And strength and honour and glory and blessing!"

When Jesus was slain and shed his blood, he received the
seven package inheritance from Satan who had stolen it from

Adam. Jesus loved us so much that he shared the inheritance with us and gave us all that the father gave him. This is your full package and you should be experiencing the fullness of your inheritance.

Matthew 28:18-20
Then Jesus came to them and said, "All authority in heaven and on earth has been given to me. Therefore go and make disciples of all nations, baptising them in the name of the Father and of the Son and of the Holy Spirit, and teaching them to obey everything I have commanded you. And surely I am with you always, to the very end of the age."

Romans 8:17
Now if we are children, then we are heirs—heirs of God and co-heirs with Christ, if indeed we share in his sufferings in order that we may also share in his glory.

A: POWER

We are not weak to the kingdom of darkness. What you are going through will not kill you for he that is in you is greater than he that is in the world.

1 John 4:4
You, dear children, are from God and have overcome them, because the one who is in you is greater than the one who is in the world.

The same spirit that raised Jesus from the dead dwells in you. All the power of God is in you child of God.

Romans 8:11
But if the Spirit of Him that raised up Jesus from the dead dwell in you, He that raised up Christ from the dead shall also quicken your mortal bodies by His Spirit that dwelleth in you.

Paul knew this hence he was not afraid even when he was pushed to the corner. He knew the power inside him was going to overcome the outside forces coming against him.

2nd corinthians 4:8-10
We are hard pressed on every side, but not crushed; perplexed, but not in despair; persecuted, but not abandoned; struck down, but not destroyed. We always carry around in our body the death of Jesus, so that the life of Jesus may also be revealed in our body.

When all hell breaks loose on you and you are afflicted, release this power through prayers. As you pray, the power from within you is released to change the environment around you.

James 5:13
Is any among you afflicted? let him pray.

James 5:16
The earnest (heartfelt, continued) prayer of a righteous man makes tremendous power available [dynamic in its working].

You have been given the privilege of the name of Jesus. All power is also there and as you use his name, all demons bow.

Pray in the spirit and use the name of Jesus.

Luke 10:17-19
The seventy-two returned with joy and said, "Lord, even the demons submit to us in your name."
He replied, "I saw Satan fall like lightning from heaven. I have given you authority to trample on snakes and scorpions and to overcome all the power of the enemy; nothing will harm you.

Also, speak the word of God over your situation for that's the power that holds the universe.
Take advantage of the power made available to you child of God and rise above your circumstance for it's part of your inheritance package.

Hebrews 1:3
who being the brightness of His glory and the express image of His person, and **upholding all things by the word of His power,** when He had by Himself purged our sins, sat down at the right hand of the Majesty on high,

B: RICHES

Just because we are God's children we should not live in poverty. Don't buy the devil's lie that you should survive and endure on your way to heaven. Others look to the day Jesus will come or they will go to heaven and live in the city of gold. If God lives in a city built with gold, don't you think he wants his children to enjoy gold on earth? It's God's will we prosper, settle that early for this is part of the inheritance package.

3rd John 1:2
Beloved, I pray that you may prosper in all things and be in health, just as your soul prospers.

If you don't take advantage of it, you will regret your days on earth like Lazarus as you wait to go to heaven. Money is important because it's a tool and a means of exchange. You need it to get the products and services for your comfortable living on earth. It's the love of money that causes people to do evil. Actually, in their aim to get money no matter what, they get out of the way of faith.

1st timothy 6:10
For the love of money is the root of all evil: which while some coveted after, they have erred from the faith, and pierced themselves through with many sorrows.

1st Timothy 6:17
Command those who are rich in this present world not to be arrogant nor to put their hope in wealth, which is so uncertain, but to put their hope in God, who richly provides us with everything for our enjoyment.

The spirit of mammon is a wicked spirit that uses money as a medium to hold people as slaves.

Matthew 6:24
No one can serve two masters; for either he will hate the one and love the other, or else he will be loyal to the one and despise the other. You cannot serve God and mammon.

You can be free from all these when you take the promise of God and believe God to deliver your inheritance of riches. He is a father, he knows you need money and he will deliver it to you.

This way you will have peace and showcase the glory of God. Poverty does not glorify God, it's prosperity that does.

Psalms 35:27

Let them shout for joy and rejoice, who favour my vindication and want what is right for me; Let them say continually, "Let the Lord be magnified, who delights and takes pleasure in the prosperity of His servant."

CHAPTER TWO: WISDOM AND STRENGTH

A: WISDOM

Wisdom is the ability to put knowledge to work so that it produces results. Too much knowledge only puffs up but knowledge put into practice will deliver and that is wisdom.

Matthew 11:19

God's wisdom, however, is shown to be true by its results.

Wisdom is the main thing to go for in the kingdom. It will give you results of long life, riches, and all you desire.

Proverbs 4:7-9
Wisdom is the principal thing; therefore get wisdom: and with all thy getting get understanding.
 Exalt her, and she shall promote thee: she shall bring thee to honour, when thou dost embrace her.
 She shall give to thine head an ornament of grace: a crown of glory shall she deliver to thee.

When God gave Solomon a blank cheque, he asked for wisdom and it brought him all other things that he didn't ask for.

1st king 3:10-12
The LORD was happy that Solomon asked for wisdom. So God said to him, "You did not ask for long life and riches for yourself. You did not ask for the death of your enemies. You asked for the wisdom to listen and make the right decisions. So I will give you what you asked for. I will make you wise

and intelligent. I will make you wiser than anyone who ever lived or ever will live. And I will also give you what you did not ask for. You will have riches and honour all your life. There will be no other king in the world as great as you.

Wisdom is a person, Jesus. When you spend time with the Lord, he will show you what to do and you will always have the answer to all problems. Wisdom is the ability to solve problems. There is no problem that Jesus saw that he didn't solve.
He was never stranded but ever above circumstances. When you operate by the wisdom of God, you will have all the answers to every challenge in your life.

1st Corinthians 1:30
But because of Him are ye in Christ Jesus, who from God is made unto us wisdom and righteousness, and sanctification and redemption.

B: STRENGTH

It's our fathers will to have strength for long life. Long life is your portion therefore if you thought your days are over, life has just begun for you. As days go, so do the world's strength but God has decreed that as your days increase, so your strength increases. Therefore, the more they think you are getting older, the more you should be full of strength.

Deuteronomy 33:25
as thy days, so shall thy strength be.

Caleb was a man that enjoyed this inheritance package. When Joshua was getting old and yet there was more inheritance to get, Caleb was getting more strength with time.

Joshua 13:1

When Joshua had grown old, the Lord said to him, "You are now very old, and there are still very large areas of land to be taken over.

He was eighty five years old and yet so strong that he went to fight for his inheritance. Many at that age are already walking with sticks, retired and seeing no hope for life. They are only waiting for death to transit them home.

Joshua 14:6-15
Now the people of Judah approached Joshua at Gilgal, and Caleb son of Jephunneh the Kenizzite said to him, "You know what the Lord said to Moses the man of God at Kadesh Barnea about you and me. I was forty years old when Moses the servant of the Lord sent me from Kadesh Barnea to explore the land. And I brought him back a report according to my convictions, but my fellow Israelites who went up with me made the hearts of the people melt in fear. I, however, followed the Lord my God wholeheartedly. So on that day Moses swore to me, 'The land on which your feet have

walked will be your inheritance and that of your children forever, because you have followed the Lord my God wholeheartedly.'

"Now then, just as the Lord promised, he has kept me alive for forty-five years since the time he said this to Moses, while Israel moved about in the wilderness. _So here I am today, eighty-five years old_! I am still as strong today as the day Moses sent me out; I'm just as vigorous to go out to battle now as I was then. Now give me this hill country that the Lord promised me that day. You yourself heard then that the Anakites were there and their cities were large and fortified, but, the Lord helping me, I will drive them out just as he said."

Then Joshua blessed Caleb son of Jephunneh and gave him Hebron as his inheritance. So Hebron has belonged to Caleb son of Jephunneh the Kenizzite ever since, because he followed the Lord, the God of Israel, wholeheartedly. (Hebron used to be called Kiriath Arba after Arba, who was the greatest man among the Anakites.)

Caleb was in the old testament and we are in the new with better promises. We should have more of what Caleb had for we have the spirit of God living in us.

Hebrews 8:6
But as it is, Christ has acquired a [priestly] ministry which is more excellent [than the old Levitical priestly ministry], for He is the Mediator (Arbiter) of a better covenant [uniting God and man], which has been enacted and rests on better promises.

Partake of the Lord's body for Adam and Eve died by eating, you can have the life of Christ by eating also. The ways of God look simple and foolish but they have power so that all Glory can go back to God.

John 6:54-55
Whoever eats My flesh and drinks My blood has eternal life, and I will raise him up at the last day. For My flesh is food indeed, and My blood is drink indeed. He who eats My flesh and drinks My blood abides in Me, and I in him.

CHAPTER THREE: HONOUR AND GLORY

A: HONOUR

Shame is from the kingdom of darkness but honour is God's plan for your life. We all start with lives full of shame for that's what Satan offers but when we come to God's kingdom, he takes away that garment of shame and clothes us with honour.

Colosians 1:13
For he has rescued us from the dominion of darkness and brought us into the kingdom of the Son he loves.

Isaiah 61:3
To console those who mourn in Zion,
To give them beauty for ashes(shame),
The oil of joy for mourning,
The garment of praise for the spirit of heaviness;
That they may be called trees of righteousness,
The planting of the Lord, that He may be glorified."

B: GLORY

it's God's will that our lives reflect his glory. When Jesus saw a blind man and the disciples tried to ask whose sin it was, Jesus saw an opportunity to showcase the father's glory by restoring the sight of the man.

John 9:1-7

Now as Jesus passed by, He saw a man who was blind from birth. And His disciples asked Him, saying, "Rabbi, who sinned, this man or his parents, that he was born blind?" **Jesus answered, "Neither this man nor his parents sinned, but that the works of God should be revealed in him.** must work the works of Him who sent Me while it is day; the night is coming when no one can work. As long as I am in the world, I am the light of the world."
When He had said these things, He spat on the ground and made clay with the saliva; and He anointed the eyes of the blind man with the clay. And He said to him, "Go, wash in the pool of Siloam" (which is translated, Sent). So he went and washed, and came back seeing.

When Lazarus was dead and all were mourning, he saw an opportunity to showcase the glory of God by raising him from the dead.

John 11:1-4
Now a certain man was sick, Lazarus of Bethany, the town of Mary and her sister Martha. It was that Mary who anointed the Lord with fragrant oil and wiped His feet with her hair, whose brother Lazarus was sick. Therefore the sisters sent to Him, saying, **"Lord, behold, he whom You love is sick." When Jesus heard that, He said, "This sickness is not unto death, but for the glory of God, that the Son of God may be glorified through it."**

John 11:38-44
Then Jesus, again groaning in Himself, came to the tomb. It was a cave, and a stone lay against it. Jesus said, "Take away the stone."
Martha, the sister of him who was dead, said to Him, "Lord, by this time there is a stench, for he has been dead for four days."

Jesus said to her, "Did I not say to you that if you would believe you would see the glory of God?" Then they took away the stone from the place where the dead man was lying. And Jesus lifted up His eyes and said, "Father, I thank You that You have heard Me. And I know that You always hear Me, but because of the people who are standing by I said this, that they may believe that You sent Me." Now when He had said these things, He cried with a loud voice, "Lazarus, come forth!" And he who had died came out bound hand and foot with graveclothes, and his face was wrapped with a cloth. Jesus said to them, "Loose him, and let him go."

Whatever challenge that is facing you, it's a platform for God to show his glory. When you see a goliath before you making people scared, be like David who saw a chance to prove that God lives.

1st samuel 17:45-50
David said to the Philistine, "You come against me with sword and spear and javelin, but I come against you in the name of the Lord Almighty, the God of the armies of Israel, whom you have defied. This day the Lord will deliver you

into my hands, and I'll strike you down and cut off your head. **This very day I will give the carcasses of the Philistine army to the birds and the wild animals, and _the whole world will know that there is a God in Israel_.** All those gathered here will know that it is not by sword or spear that the Lord saves; for the battle is the Lord's, and he will give all of you into our hands."

As the Philistine moved closer to attack him, David ran quickly toward the battle line to meet him. Reaching into his bag and taking out a stone, he slung it and struck the Philistine on the forehead. The stone sank into his forehead, and he fell facedown on the ground.

So David triumphed over the Philistine with a sling and a stone; without a sword in his hand he struck down the Philistine and killed him.

CHAPTER FOUR: BLESSING

The blessing of God is that power that attracts all you need to live a successful life. That is what God gives his children and in their lifetime, it attracts everything they need for a glorious life at the right time.

Proverbs 10:22
The blessing of the Lord makes one rich,
And He adds no sorrow with it.

Deuteronomy 8:18
"And you shall remember the Lord your God, for it is He who gives you power to get wealth, that He may establish His covenant which He swore to your fathers, as it is this day.

It was the blessing that God gave to Adam and Eve. It was that power that enabled them to be fruitful.

Genesis 1:28
God blessed them and said to them, "Be fruitful and increase in number; fill the earth and subdue it. Rule over the fish in the sea and the birds in the sky and over every living creature that moves on the ground."

It was the blessing that God gave Abraham and he that was barren was able to have a child and gain wealth that he was admired by the people of the world.

Genesis 12:3
The Lord had said to Abram, "Go from your country, your people and your father's household to the land I will show you.
"I will make you into a great nation,
and I will bless you;
I will make your name great,
and you will be a blessing.
I will bless those who bless you,
and whoever curses you I will curse;
and all peoples on earth
will be blessed through you."

Genesis 13:2
And Abram was very rich in cattle, in silver, and in gold.

Genesis 21:1-7

Now the Lord was gracious to Sarah as he had said, and the Lord did for Sarah what he had promised. Sarah became pregnant and bore a son to Abraham in his old age, at the very time God had promised him. Abraham gave the name Isaac to the son Sarah bore him. When his son Isaac was eight days old, Abraham circumcised him, as God commanded him. Abraham was a hundred years old when his son Isaac was born to him.

Sarah said, "God has brought me laughter, and everyone who hears about this will laugh with me." And she added, "Who would have said to Abraham that Sarah would nurse children? Yet I have borne him a son in his old age."

It doesn't matter how dry it is in your life, the blessing will produce the power you need to see the wilderness turned into a fruitful land.

Ephesians 1:3
Praise be to the God and Father of our Lord Jesus Christ, who has blessed us in the heavenly realms with every spiritual blessing in Christ.

CONCLUSION

The father has given you his spirit who will help you to take full advantage of your inheritance. Follow the leading of the spirit of God within you and you shall be an envy to the people of the world.

Romans 8:14
For those who are led by the Spirit of God are the children of God.

The holy spirit has the seven sides of the inheritance with him and he will lead you in the way of the inheritance.

Isaiah 11:2-3
The Spirit of the Lord shall rest upon Him,
The Spirit of wisdom and understanding,
The Spirit of counsel and might,
The Spirit of knowledge and of the fear of the Lord.
 His delight is in the fear of the Lord,
And He shall not judge by the sight of His eyes,

Nor decide by the hearing of His ears.

He knows the father's plan for your life, he will guide you to enjoy the inheritance. He is your guide through life, only have an obedient heart.

1st Corinthians 2:9-10
But as it is written:

"Eye has not seen, nor ear heard,
Nor have entered into the heart of man
The things which God has prepared for those who love Him."

But God has revealed them to us through His Spirit. For the Spirit searches all things, yes, the deep things of God.

JOHN 13:17

NOW THAT YOU KNOW THESE THINGS, YOU WILL BE BLESSED IF YOU DO THEM.

More Grace on you as you enjoy your inheritance as a child of God and showcase your father's glory.

If you need help to study the word of God, email me at pstmaryjoy@gmail.com and I will guide you through.

To get my other books in amazon, click this link https://www.amazon.com/author/marynyandia

www.ingramcontent.com/pod-product-compliance
Lightning Source LLC
Chambersburg PA
CBHW070905220526
45466CB00005B/2138